The Moral Theology of the Devil/ Clothed With The Sun

Linda Kemp

Leafe Press

Published by Leafe Press
Nottingham, England.
www.leafepress.org

ISBN: 978-1-7397213-8-1

The Moral Theology of the Devil/ Clothed With The Sun

"the will that is the captive of its own desire cannot accept the seeds of an unfamiliar truth"

Thomas Merton

to ride
reality steps in
experience
this
soiled
knoll
of never un-
named & simple
societal swirls
a blessing
proof of
a blue carpet
green canopy
an alien existence
of finitude
disposed
of rites
temper
a river
seized &
broken elbows
arms of
ecstasy dotting
the horizon
join
confusion
the ray
blots what
the graven
to idolise
inalienable echo

*

vitals
interrupt
a dialogue of hills
the will of
whatever realisation
dips in the drive
seeds
domineering
the impressionable
affability of not
wakening until
uneventful trust
unfurls a lovely
rain across
the sea
light
food of
will
pleasure of
demand
& hey
task is mere
asking to be
the step
permanence
properly speaking
direction
the diurnal
breeze
tolerating duty
root

*

everything
that is rather
ear the new
mind the broken
step
to
misgiving
knowing
who no longer
steps aside
the knowing of
relationship
in whose house
the chimney-stacks
shelves
selves
whistling
hi-ho
the ego shuffles
worn &
coat peg shining
compatible
cold
with a sip
it was
& this
slaking body dual
offence
know everything is
the consecrate
the dwells
sings
certain in the perfect

sure
separation
in five steps
stinking outside
haptic
& glorious

*

the perilous hands
subdivide
rooting the country
less like
yellow flowers
faces
the looking up & saints
beauty in hills
uninterrupted
sanctity
tears
create a truth
eye
the long run
coastal
fidelity &
mystery
no more nailing
ships
to sails
planning liberty
elides
freedom masking grief
outside probability
rest in
thereafter
sheets winding
a game
except
in discovery

*

true to
concept
hacking through
vapidity
an ode
clothing
the veils with clouds
the hay
beauty
waning with contact
haptic & happy
bending
to bring vital stone
to ground
trembling contemplatives
lift
missional appearances
dash to
water
gratuity
divine bee
mirrored
asleep
formally falling so
complete
reach
hitherto outwith
such & such
glow with confusion
the bulbous sleep of
order
the disposal of
entertaining
friends in the secret comfort of
resting
silence is

*

less them
affect & know
the snow steps of
living death
the habit of fortitude
lain
labouring in
knotty desire
the wings
longer
sailing stubbornly
through night
air
touch is-
olates
infancy creeping though
kinds of dullness
matters
plunging through
solitude
descent into the other
often solitary
personalisation
exchange
for togetherness
tiptoe
across the landing
smelling
lobster
empty
conventional pots
sound painless
mere sufficiency

washes
the burden
judging
joy
not by conviction
competitiveness folds
away

*

sleep
polishes
the dust
shows face
the external
hiring an empty hall
raising
funds
the suffering
a green line
flashing into the dark horizon
towering
over irrelevant
sheep
chewing
empty discovery

*

dishes stack
possessions close the door
woken into
almost
spitting dark
spirits
capabilities
showing up
sharing
activities as accusations
the weather-beaten
fields
a damp nose
knowing how to
always
if in the fruit
the terminal
self-sufficiency
of serving
ends
the walk to know
subsists
relating
going into under
remonstrating
throwing tables
refined
in murderous union
stop
tiptoeing
out in otherness
steep cruelties
bend
weeping
the broom brings home

our us
again
because
slipping into principles
undoes the doing
demanding to be
other
suffers
& it in while
slows the
stands &
unable to step over
reaches under
into the private
driving

*

untether
into idleness
the silence of attachments
releasing into
comradely sharing
promoting uselessness
instead of work
lifting hours into
units
the dissolving into
sensing
roaring with the insult
of finding
finally
not in doing
status
lies silent
appetite dies
just because
unwrapping
sandwiches in greaseproof paper
talking silly
songs &
subjugating solitude
for
ordinate norms
blink
& be fully disposed

*

systems
order
& opportunity manifests as
thinginess
the final fact of
taking bad care of
occupation
squatting in a tent &
hating everyone
contemplating
complacency
in everyone
the conviction of convicting
everyone
except friends
the irrelevancy
impractical action
sneezing over
conclusions
the wipe-clean
get-rich-quick
sign of nothing
happening
accepting
by faith alone
the stars do not love
but tell the times
without evidence
the regeneration
effective in affecting
pieces of parts
no one is counting
children's eyes
limbs

graves
attachments
torn
the sea
the sea

*

testimony winds down
opinions fail
to humble themselves
houses
walls
indifference in the face
outrage
has everyone stood up here
intending to feel
first the never
then the tough solitude of saying
the wipe-clean beginning
knowing you can never
not know again
seeing this
sharing
honesty is learned
from balance
the tough application of admiration
looking up & learning
peculiar combinations
of ambition
stubborn out-group praise
the enthusiasm of enthusiastically
rejecting the abstract for the living
embodying the field

*

rectitude comforting
risk appeals
to campaigning others
sitting in a lift
ringing
confirmation of loss
bringing struggle &
unthinkable identities
not to be saved
but to be seen
witness is no longer
good enough
as good taste
suffers in the viewing
the newly new lifting out of dust
the dusty others
the future present
ceasing
reason
there is not necessarily
menace in having
but
unwillingly yielding
overs dependence
out of autonomy
self-determination foxes
servitude
knowing not to know these justifications
service others
the wipe-clean
as self-disgusted

*

fear is war
our selves & other
easing
eating to exaggeration
intensifying
until evil
to be rid of
eye
confusion is total
the distain of condensation
the root
compassionate & seeking
wrong-headedness
the fact of politics
the circle of
these caterpillars
the cocoon of concrete
let go
pointing out exaggeration
exhortation
folly
step closer
protection risk
destroying

*

nothing but fire
history
fruits
heroism
scattering the desert
corners
the field ripe
dormice &
suckling
serpents
sleep through tedium &
disconnect
the ariel loving under guidance
gauze underneath
accepting
nothing to hold
no matter
how tight the heart
fills
the fire conceives
the rope
tilting across stonework
the smooth rubble of redevelopment
the truth of lies
the bullishness of leadership &
knowing what is wrong & backing it
do not sleep tight tonight or ever
friends
the knowing what is wrong & shaping it
the take-home pay of leadership &
battlegrounds
shame knowing what is right &
leaving it
imagining how to say it & not saying it

leaping over rivers & not bridging it
looking like you know & not knowing it
creating a likeness of an image & promoting it
the intellect is simply just not
good enough to mine the
depravity of knowing & just walking it
racing to the edge & then not
sailing it
looking certain & then speaking of a rectitude
assuring of solidarity then not giving it
waking up & knowing it
wrong every one of us &
giving up
violence helps our insecurity
not giving it

*

accountancy attempts to integrate
mystery with limit
beyond erasure
cities
utilities
the exceedingly harmful
misleading not knowing
policy decisions
censorious unity
blocks
who dwells
directly conditioned
by reflex
the tightrope of
drops
the precarity of higher principles
reconstituting activity
the rational
look beyond
to characteristics
revolving yes
to those who hurt
look
yesterday is always must
escaping
justice
a step
to relief &
fluid moss
the rising sea of definitions
the dogmatic promise of drowning
before knowing what is right
& funding it
shaping it out of discourse doesn't alter it
materially

rewriting solitude into solidarity doesn't
activate the promise into terminology
even phenomenology is an empty lie
but humility formulates
sits with apprehension
shows
definition in obscurity
lights the medium
squat into bothering
& finding begins
switch

*

really the subsisting
illusions
hear agape
but secrecy
trades contemporaneity
sameness
freights
bothersomeness wanting
to be different
sticking labels into shared clothes
ironing out
enough to reproduce
without commonality
the institutional misuse
communing
the selling of education
counting on
or the first
or none
sticking to a theoretical framework &
milking
heartfelt effort for exchange
no one lives at home anymore
understand
rating
is a cost
raking the hearth
shaking fists at unseen gods
the sounds of bells
fearing everything
sleighs
promotion
compelling arguments
pave the
lupins lilac

recent ploughed fields &
the absorbency of
flying deep into s. america to
taste a revolution
in translation
look out
watery sacrifice
the broken duties
formally take place without
obscurity
the knee-deep compromising
keeps the scuttle
subjective
kneeling at the cross & angry
faces ticking
boxes
the annual resolution
of doing wrong & rewarding it
face up in the river &
garlanding it   O
revolutionary species
walk in the image
of blood & labour
even
told of sanctity
grasping at since
though language
heaps
everything
there goes importance
weeping
veiling something unmeant
into tiny rowing boats &
sitting on the river
weaving in absence
it is fitting
to talk
without the object

sitting below the river
a god
looking at the slowly moving hands
& knowing most secrets
hide in offices
under water
torpedoed
shrugging &
encouraging further sharing until
someone forgets to turn the lights
down
the great glory of instrumentalisation
shudders into silence
the palaeontologists' predictions
warm into futures
the divine
flickering
please
being poor facilitates a movement
through entryways
over robes
the supernatural hearing of the listening
word

*

twenty-six varieties of selfishness
sit quickly
if perhaps
avarice
sloth
the ease of slipping quietly
alone
to breeze through country houses
spotting historical significance
marvelling at property rights
& enslavement
subterfuge is the needy
doing
landing without medical supplies
accepting poverty
& worrying
for rent
between the material & absolute
penny
pride
swims
fields
horses
& steam trains
perfection unifies the past &
offers
prevention as deepest need
the seat of knowing
learning is not
being right
but knowing what is known is doing wrong
walking through the house at night
sounding
friendship with all the people known &

unknown across a life
& feeling right
looking in the speckled mirror &
seeing everyone
too ardent
becomes an obstacle
opacity slips into shoes
squeaks through night
the final
in bed
& looking up to see yourself
looking at yourself through
the mirror of your own eyes
but younger
justifies a life
only humility will recognise

*

consequence needs
accusation
with no other concern
the confidence to step
into shoes
wide enough to accommodate
an untreated bunion
the freedom
wiggling toes at the foot of the bed
insuperable
needs hermits
dry
to think to book
to mediate
activity to fruit
abandonment is not the will
habits
wavering trust to own
yet
convincing the congratulatory
crowd into order
re-routes license
to pull the sheets
deficiencies
deliberately to ease
difficulties
do not really want to do
consists
travel is amiable
without
happiness
wrapping over remnants
performed as
reminiscence
looking over lakes &
knowing no one sacrifices

this way
without cost
the understanding moan
stating
liability from resting while
applying formally correct gestures
into principles
accounting for circumstances
even the garden
perambulates politely
next-door
most brilliant scholars equating
latitude with relaxation
pleasures & a glass
ceaselessly in motion
making
involvement further away from appetite
the rush for peace
without the plurality of
difference
squawks from branches
buries a bone
recalling forbidden beginnings
the exteriority of trying
exquisite platitudes
face-down in the dirt
mysticise
the taste
attached to feeling
the longing
sips
drawing itself
into a mirror
removed so
the font is a ring
o' roses
the masks of medievalism

a parochial abstraction
a photograph resolutely facing
cowardice
detached

*

defeat infuses talk
& sails
disciplining surface
narrow
& purposeful
constant lakes
teeming with
someone doesn't know how to name
see these
listening drops to mouths
popping against the surface
boggle-eyed
& sown bafflement attuning to anything
except the crossroads
beautiful hedgerows
the wren
the reaching out
utterly relaxing until
now to know to enter
without
affections
a secret
swimming is an ecstasy
the politic of staving
privileging mute love
into obedience
if there were no job
to realise refusal is most feared
& harmless
tense with only humour
as disarmament
at one time
too involved in clarity
to wake up
within grasp

folds
a different foiling
the obviousness of setting out
to clarify
the snail of certitude
immensity
counting out instinct on the outside
as though at last
fully extent
leaning into the exterior
doors
chattering
on one condition
given
against caution
plumbs acceptance
resolute in
emptying laundry
the inarticulate wash
counting out
immaculate baseboards
without limit
stands among
a lifetime
lush & desolate
mortification
swaying in the close
of being told
finally
it's fine
it's not
it's
the cold night call of being told
& over
there the words return
solitary & with
out will
begins to seep

soil
helplessness through the wilderness
the wild quickens
knowing
not in keeping
but letting go
bringing in the private place
hungry
silence
acts of one
absorbing
maps into dependence

*

the necessity of needing
knows the contemplative
exuberance of tone
speckled
a good swim
the excess of an orderly exit
cold
alone
steps into not quite true
the beautiful
attention
speaking
attachment
suffering
always as if only
joy

Acknowledgements

The excerpts 'vitals', 'the perilous hands', 'true to' and 'really the sub-sisting' were previously published in Shearsman vol. 143 & 144.
The excerpts 'untether', 'rectitude comforting' and 'defeat infuses talk' were previously published in Litter. With thanks to the editors.